What A Life!

2005

What A Life!

A Kaleidoscope of
Rajinder Puri's Cartoons

Partha Chatterjee • Arvindar Singh

NIYOGI
BOOKS

Published by
NIYOGI BOOKS
Block D, Building No. 77,
Okhla Industrial Area, Phase-I,
New Delhi-110 020, INDIA
Tel: 91-11-26816301, 26818960
Email: niyogibooks@gmail.com
Website: www.niyogibooksindia.com

Editor: Jayalakshmi Sengupta
Design: Nabanita Das

ISBN: 978-93-86906-05-2
Publication: 2017

Printed at: Niyogi Offset Pvt. Ltd., New Delhi, India

To all Cartoonists
whose work upheld the values
of Liberty, Fraternity and Equality.

Swiftian Satirist

Rajinder Puri (20 September 1934–16 February 2015) was an exceptional cartoonist and political columnist with a marked gift for incisive drawing and writing. His work has a directness and purity of purpose, seldom seen in the oeuvre of Indian cartoonists or columnists. There were the likes of O.V. Vijayan, who could draw and write expressively, but none had Puri's bent for savage satire. It no doubt, had a connection with the Partition of India, an event without a parallel in 20th-century history, where 1.8 million people—Hindus, Muslims, Sikhs—were

massacred. It scarred the psyche of people in India and Pakistan, and memories of psychological and physical wounds inflicted on each other survive to this day. Puri was only 13 when he came to Delhi with his family from Karachi, but the cataclysmic happening was to mark him for life, as it did millions of others.

He was 22 when he finished his Masters in History from St. Stephen's College, Delhi University. He had already begun to reveal a talent for satirical drawing and writing. It was a matter of time before he plunged into a full-time career as a cartoonist and journalist. He had also met the dynamic socialist, Ram Manohar Lohia, whose thoughts were to remain with the aspiring tyro for the rest of his life. Puri, carried within himself, till the end, Lohia's scepticism about the Congress's intentions to rule India fairly and bring succour to the poor and needy.

His artistic credentials—the expression would have embarrassed him no end—were established soon enough. His drawing had raw power and a quality of expression that at once brought two artists to mind—Jonathan Swift (1667–1745) and Honoré Daumier (1808–1879). The first, an Englishman, wrote the savage satire, *Gulliver's Travels,* and the second was a Frenchman, a cartoonist and painter of profound humane qualities.

Swift, probably, opened for Puri, the doors of realisation about greed and avarice being fundamental traits in human beings, and Daumier unlocked the varied possibilities of using lines in the expression of ideas and emotions—more so, those associated with satire and trenchant social criticism.

His ability to use the grotesque through line, and later tone, may possibly owe something to a viewing of reproductions and possibly originals of the medieval Dutch master, Hieronymus Bosch, and the early 20th-century German cartoonist and painter, George Grosz.

Puri would have been alarmed at such cultural heavyweights being dragged in to justify the quality of his cartoons and caricatures. He was a lifelong debunker of so-called high culture, which for him had its roots in inexplicable snobbery. He once wrote in the visitor's book, after seeing the exhibition of a well-regarded modern Indian painter, that even he [Puri] could understand the paintings!

He learned the ropes of his profession when in England, working with *The Manchester Guardian* and also the *Glasgow Herald*. He had, in an unguarded moment, during a tea-session, confessed to have seen the art of the classical and modern European masters while in England. It was then that he met leading English cartoonists like Ronald Searle, Osbert Lancaster, Gerald Scarfe, and others.

He was instinctively averse to 'high culture' and its proponents though he responded keenly to Hindustani music, both vocal and instrumental. Always the champion of the underdog, he spoke glowingly of the khayal singing of Ustad Chote Ghulam Ali Khan, who also hailed from Kasur (now in Pakistan) like his illustrious senior Ustad Bade Ghulam Ali Khan.

Puri narrated a hilarious story about the sitar maestro Pandit Ravi Shankar's first concert at the Harivallabh music festival in Jalandhar in the early 1950s. The largely rustic Panjabi audience was musically well informed but a little too generous in the use of choice expletives to express their appreciation. Ravi Shankar warmed up quickly and played a series of difficult *taans* with supreme confidence and the audience showered him with colourful four-letter words expressing approval. The sitarist was taken aback. As he was getting ready for another piece, he asked his pupil Jhinghan, in soto-voce, if he played all that badly. Jhinghan, Puri's college friend said, 'Guruji you are playing brilliantly!'

'Then why are they abusing me?'

Suppressing a smile, he replied, 'No! Not at all, they are showing their love and admiration for your masterly performance!'

Puri's writing was as biting as his drawing. He was at his best, in short pieces on topical subjects. Vinod Mehta, fearless former editor of *Outlook,* got him to do Bull's Eye, a short satirical weekly piece with a matching illustration. By then, Puri, the alleged Luddite, had learned to use the personal computer and its graphic possibility in his unique way. The piece in the following paragraph was written in his column on 13 December 1999, five years after the demolition of the Babri Masjid, in Ayodhya, Uttar Pradesh, by the satellites of the Bharatiya Janata Party, namely, the Vishwa Hindu Parishad, the Bajrang Dal, the Rashtriya Swayamsevak Sangh. The truth was murkier than what met the eye. Puri's take on it is simultaneously very angry and funny:

> Last week's grand bash in Mulayam's house to celebrate his son's [Akhilesh Yadav] wedding provided some indication. Mulayam, who defended Babri Masjid and ordered the police to shoot karsevaks, warmly hugged Kalyan [Singh], whose mob killed Muslims and demolished the Masjid. Laloo, [Yadav] messiah of Muslims, hugged Kalyan, the saviour of Hindus.
>
> Laloo said: 'Kalyan is our friend. The people of Bihar are calling him.'
>
> Kalyan said: 'If the PM can abandon the temple issue, who am I to persist with it?'
>
> The PM never supported the Masjid's demolition.

Puri continues in the next paragraph,

> Never mind if Hindus and Muslims were killed in the hatred unleashed by these leaders. Now there's peace among them. And that living insult to Karl Marx, H.S. Surjeet, has blessed it. 'The third front will again emerge,' he said.

Puri, considered politicians, regardless of their affiliations, to be harbingers of evil; ones responsible for the slaughter of innocents and the looting of the Indian nation and its natural resources.

It is important to pause and discuss other contemporaries, who were very gifted in their own way.

R.K. Laxman, was, by far, the most famous of his peers. His wit was somewhat like that of his novelist elder brother, R.K. Narayan—droll, playful, gentle, rarely, if ever, angry. In the Common Man—an ongoing character for his daily pocket cartoon—and, on occasions, larger editorial cartoons modelled on the average middle-class man, Laxman attained lasting fame. His bespectacled, bald, dhoti-clad, slightly befuddled character was an observer of rather than a participant in the important and not-so-important events of daily life; he was neither a radical nor a crusader.

O.V. Vijayan's cartoons were political but without the contentious wit that characterised Puri's work. Abu [Abraham] had a lyrical, whimsical streak in him, like his younger colleague, E.P. Unny has these days. Sudhir Dar, in his best work, had a quiet, mischievous sense of humour. The gifted Mario Miranda had sparkle and optimism, but he wasn't a daily newspaper cartoonist really. Not one of these individuals was politically committed in the same fiery way as Rajinder Puri; they had other interests apart from cartooning and, on occasion, also wrote. Puri, through his cartoons and columns lived entirely for politics—for him, it was the rendering of a public service. Puri saw his writing and cartooning as vehicles for spreading public awareness on burning issues of the day.

In his collection of essays titled, *India: The Wasted Years*, 1969–1975, he wrote the following about the Emergency, soon to be declared by Prime Minister Indira Gandhi, of the Congress government at the centre.

> Landlords and labourers, capitalists and workers, students and teachers, Sikhs and Muslims—each class and community in India today is victim of its own grievance, a strident, and sometime violent champion of its own cause. Each section of society has its own private grouse, but, inexorably, all are finding a common cause in their hatred of authority at all levels. The Government is becoming the common enemy, and the police is a common target of public wrath.

The 19 month Emergency, declared in June 1975, marked him for life, as it did many at that time. He became the founder general secretary of the Janata Party, which defeated the Congress in the national elections, but soon the party became a hotbed of intrigue as personal ambitions of politicians clashed.

Rajinder Puri also wrote a good number of books like *Crisis of Conscience* (1969), *India: The Wasted Years* (1975), *The Recovery of India* (1992), *Bull's Eye* (2004), and *A Tale of Two Countries* (2008).

We focus on two of his works here *Crisis of Conscience* and *Bull's Eye*.

Crisis of Conscience deals with the 1969 split in the Congress Party. On 12 July 1969, the Congress had nominated Lok Sabha Speaker, Neelam Sanjiva Reddy, for the post of

President of India, but Indira Gandhi had him defeated by appealing for a conscience vote for the independent candidate, former Vice President, V.V. Giri. The Congress split into two factions Congress (ruling) and Congress (organisation) in November 1969.

Thus Puri's book was timely and hard-hitting. He once mentioned that he had actually been commissioned by the *Statesman* to write the book, but when the manuscript was put up to the newspaper it was felt to be too hot for publication. Puri then sold his car and published it himself.

Puri's portrayal of the various political leaders of the period is both hilarious as well as spot on in its accuracy of their various characteristics. For example his description of Morarji Desai gives the true flavour of the man as many, who knew Morarji, will grasp easily. At one place he says:

> [P]erhaps, to be charitable he is not so much the simpleton he appears to be. It is just that his responses to people, to political people, are muddled, and it seems that he often misses the nuance of a gesture thrown out by friends and foes alike. Very much like the good bridge player, playing by obsolete conventions, missing out on calls, and muffing chances, but yet in the playing of the hand having finesse, an authority born out of mildewed memories of old victories.

The idiosyncrasies of all other characters are equally well depicted—the deviousness of Y.B. Chavan (who let down the Congress old guard by doing a double dance and then siding with Mrs Gandhi), the earthiness of K. Kamaraj (who wielded an uncommon influence over men and matters till his fall), and the unpredictability of Mrs Indira Gandhi (who did not hesitate to use the worst Machiavellian tactics to achieve her ends; Puri describes her 'cute Frenchy voice rising to a slight nasal intonation at the higher pitch').

The volume also contains a prophetic statement on the danger of a dictatorial government under Mrs Gandhi taking over the country, which happened 6 years later with the declaration of Emergency in 1975. If Indira came back with a thumping mandate, he had warned—as it happened in 1971—democracy could well give way to dictatorship when people`s aspirations were not fulfilled. Such was the sharp intuition Puri had of upcoming political events.

Bull's Eye published in 2004, a good 35 years after *Crisis of Conscience,* is of a different genre although the fire in his written work remains the same. It is compilation of his columns published in *Outlook* magazine in the late 1990s and early 2000s. One column entitled 'Modern Media' has Puri as a reporter going to a drought-hit village in Saurashtra to interview the villagers about the national crisis, which is actually about cricket match fixing! The piece culminates with Puri discussing Coke and Pepsi in an appropriate spoof on the illogical and insensitive questions, often posed by television reporters.

While writing in *Outlook* on 30 September 2002, he hit out in no uncertain terms against Narendra Modi, then Chief Minister of Gujarat, by stating:

> Modi had made a highly provocative speech during his Gaurav Yatra displaying contempt, ridicule, and hatred for a religious community.

He called upon the then President Abdul Kalam to dismiss the Gujarat ministry. This is not to say that Puri pulled his punches when he came to talking about the Congress Party. On 1 November 1999, he wrote a satirical article on Nehru's 'Tryst With Destiny' speech:

> On August 14, 1947 at the stroke of the midnight hour when the conscience of leaders slept, India awoke to partition and bloodshed... the soul of a nation long suppressed was once
> more cunningly deceived.

Puri thus maintained the balance of an objective journalist. His brother Lt General Parikshit Puri (Retd) related an interesting incident that illustrates his commitment to principle. When Pran Chopra was the Editor of the *Statesman* and Puri the staff cartoonist, he found an article on the Op-Ed page totally in variance to the cartoon he had drawn

on the page opposite it. Puri protested to Chopra, who assured him it would not happen again. But this was repeated twice after this, and Puri resigned even though he was getting a salary of Rs 3,000, a princely sum in the 1960s.

He was General Secretary of the newly formed Janata Party in 1977 after the Emergency, which he largely spent underground. Prime Minister Morarji Desai, offered Puri the post of Press Secretary to the Prime Minister, a post of considerable influence that no scribe would ordinarily decline. But Puri was no ordinary scribe. He refused to accept the post as he wanted to play a political role or nothing at all.

The Janata Party split later and out of it emerged entities like the Janata Dal, Lok Dal, and most significantly the present BJP. Puri worked briefly with the Labour Cell of the BJP and realised it was not for him. He was far too independent a man to follow orders that did not make sense to him. He gave up organised politics in 1988.

He continued to crusade till the very end for social and political justice for everyone, regardless of his/her religion or economic status. He displayed a kind of continuous fearlessness that was the pride and envy of fellow journalists.

Forty years ago, his contempt for the Congress, a party he held responsible for the Partition of India, was more than offset by his admiration for Mahatma Gandhi. In an essay, 'Remembering Gandhi', he observes:

> It is tragic that since Independence a generation has been brought up in India on tales of Gandhi the man, and has been denied access to Gandhi the revolutionary. The man was killed by his enemies, and the revolutionary has been buried by his followers, but the legacy that he left his followers was too rich, the credit afforded by his goodwill too generous, for them to altogether discard his memory…As his followers rejoiced in Delhi, Gandhi fasted in Noakhali, embittered by his betrayal. He turned away without a word the All India Radio correspondent sent from Delhi to Noakhali to record his message for Independence Day. A few months later, he fell to an assassin's bullet. It was left to his followers to murder his message.

He wrote, in continuation of his crusade for justice, in his Bull's Eye column in the 21 October 2002 issue of *Outlook*. The piece was called, 'Cops at Work':

> 'Seven months have passed, we still haven't got the truth about Godhra,' I said. 'Wait for seven years,' a lawyer advised me. 'Remember the mass cremations in Punjab? Remember J. S. Khalra? More than seven years have passed. Have we got the truth?'

Jaswant Singh Khalra, head of the human rights wing of the Akali Dal was taken away by the police for issuing a press statement that stated how thousands of people under arrest had been quietly killed and cremated by the police. Khalra was made to disappear without a trace. In the same piece Puri says:

> The CBI investigations confirmed that 2,097 disappearances were accounted for in the mass cremations organised in the Amritsar district alone. The remaining 16 districts of Punjab were not investigated. The The Committee for Coordination on Disappearances in Punjab (CCDP) has documented the identities of over 1,700 of the police victims, their families, and the circumstances, which lead to their arrests, custodial deaths, and cremations. There are detailed reports of how innocents with no connection to terrorism were tortured and killed in cold blood by the police, in some cases driving their relatives to suicide or insanity.

He then comments:

> The NHRC [National Human Rights Commission] is still dawdling. Pinochet of Chile and Milosevic of Serbia were named international war criminals for crimes no worse.

Rajinder Puri, wrote in the same perceptive and outraged style, till the end. In his last piece that appeared on 13 October 2014 in the *Statesman,* he wrote of a Modi mukt or Modi-free Bharat, in the context of the political situation prevailing then. Predictably enough he never wrote for the paper again!

Drawing or writing Rajinder Puri was his own man; not always the fire and brimstone preacher as this piece may suggest, he also capable of laughing and making others laugh just for the pleasure of it.

1960–1970

SECTION–I

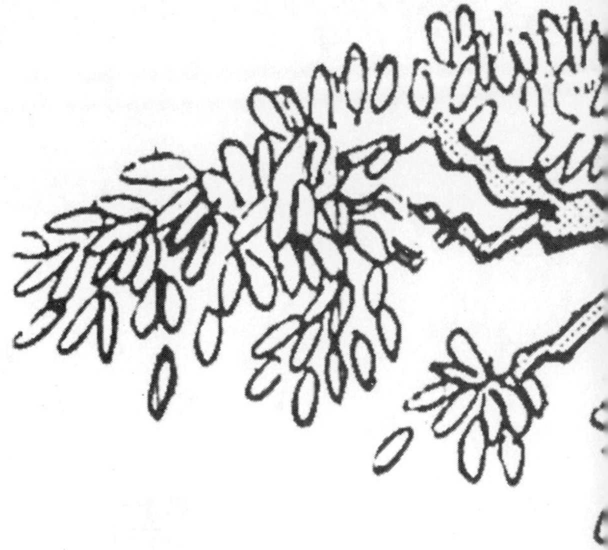

The period between 1960 to 1970 was a tumultuous phase in India, as well as the world in general. At the opening of the decade, giants like Khrushchev, Kennedy, De Gaulle, Macmillan, and Nehru dominated the international arena. Puri's cartoons covered the Cold War and the goings-on in this sphere in a subtle manner, which was to become his trademark style.

On the domestic front, Indian politics was going through an equally clamorous time. The China war of 1962, the death of Nehru, the Lal Bahadur Shastri era, the advent of Indira Gandhi as prime minister in 1966 and the Congress split of 1969 were among the principal events in India during the period. Rajinder Puri's acerbic brush captured these events with a striking impact on the reader as the years rolled by. Some cartoons in this section are from his pocket cartoons published with the byline, What A Life (W.A.L.).

"Lend me some change please, will you?"

Right: *Even a pigeon gets high on opium! (W.A.L.)*

Facing page: *It was revealed that a big amount was being spent on Prime Minister Nehru daily (Rs 25,000/-). The cartoon depicts Nehru asking Finance Minister Morarji Desai for change as he has only big currency and cannot buy the newspaper from the vendor (W.A.L.)*

"And where did you say you were last night?"

"Damn! The old girl has woken up!"

This is a spoof on various world leaders trying to bury the Commonwealth by making it irrelevant. However it refuses to die

"Bothering me with his advances?
Oh no officer, it's just that I'm in his vicinity!"

On the eve of the Sino-India conflict of 1962, Mao Zedong is seen making advances to Defence Minister V.K. Krishna Menon dressed as a woman

Today's engagement.

"We promised you Mr Vajpayee, as long as we're there you'll see few Chinese incursions!"

Right: *Vajpayee blindfolded (when he was Member of Parliament)*

Facing page: *(above) Jawaharlal Nehru, Charles De Gaulle, and Harold Macmillan depicted in a love triangle as in the Ingrid Bergman film* Goodbye Again

(below) De Gaulle and Macmillan witness the Indo-China bout as President Kennedy sits at the ticket counter

"Please, would you bend a little...?"

Nehru appeals for trade benefits from President De Gaulle of France

"...And what if there's a
power breakdown?"

Skeletons discuss the pitfalls of an electric crematorium! (W.A.L.)

"I'd like a cup of coffee. Should we stage a walk-out?"

"Angrezi men gali nikalta hai. ...

Left: *Members of Parliament want any excuse to stage a walkout! (W.A.L.)*

Right: *Nehru is confronted by a staunch Hindi supporter (W.A.L.)*

"How terrible! Indian imperialists attacked us again tomorrow morning!"

"Do something ... Fly over the affected area make a speech, appeal for funds..."

Left: *Mao Zedong cooks up an image of Indian aggression! (W.A.L.)*

Right: *A typical political appeal in India during floods. It continues to be relevant even today (W.A.L.)*

During the 1962 crisis, Mao Zedong is shown as a bull in a China shop while Nehru mans the counter

Goodbye Mr Chips

A defeat in the Gurudwara Elections spelt the decline of the Akali Dal leader, Master Tara Singh

"Remember! It is not a cold war—it is just cold up there!"

"And I can truely say that Ceylon is like a second home to me..."

"Ugh! I wish I could send your particular sweets to the Chinese soldiers."

Right: *Chinese aggression brings forth strange feelings. The quality of sweetmeats in Delhi, for example! (W.A.L.)*

Facing page: *(left) The cold climate in NEFA in the China war was a indeed one of the chief causes of our setbacks as our troops did not have adequate warm clothing (W.A.L.)*

(right) Nehru's statement in Ceylon provokes a nationalist response (W.A.L.)

"The public has no confidence left in Mr Nehru....or in the Congress.... or in any other Opposition programme..."

"Personally, if I got a crore of rupees I would feel ready to retire from politics!"

Left: *At a rally, Nath Pai of the Praja Socialist Party, which Puri renamed the Pip Squeak Party! (W.A.L.)*

Right: *The lure of money is more than the lure of power! (W.A.L.). Two politicans in a moment of candour*

A clean-up?

Nehru shown sweeping various corruption charges under the carpet. Puri's comment on the Kamaraj Plan under which senior Congress Ministers quit the government for Party work

"Who says we aren't vigilant about our defence?"

"But how ridiculous—you're just a motley crowd!"

"Since the stage is more crowded, permit me to face this side and speak...."

Right: *The travails of democracy. (W.A.L.)*

Facing page: *(above) The NEFA Report (Henderson Brooks Committee) is kept under wraps by the Nehru government. It has never been made public by successive governments*

(below) Nehru's government faces a no-confidence motion. The unity of the opposition is lost on Mr Nehru, while congressmen scrap with each other

"But I am too old to work Sir—let me stay back as minister..."

"You don't think some comrades have struck against the strike call, comrade?"

Right: *Profiles (clockwise) of Lal Bahadur Shastri, Jagjivan Ram, Morarji Desai and S.K. Patil (1963)*

Facing page: *(left) Many did not like the Kamaraj Plan (W.A.L.)*

(right) Strike by the Left Parties causes a controversy (W.A.L.)

American support—18

"Relax! Nothing will happen—people can't be more bitter than they are!"

Right: *Sugar prices cause bitterness! (W.A.L.)*

Facing page: *(above) Sheikh Abdullah was on a goodwill visit to Pakistan at Nehru's behest. President Ayub Khan is shown covering Azad Kashmir with a carpet*

(below) Lyndon Johnson and Mao Zedong kid around with Southeast Asia

"Be patient if the water supply is cut—just remember your bus isn't coming either!"

"We must respond to the PM's call for work—now what should we lobby for? A cabinet ministership"

Left: *The usual problems of the bus commuter (W.A.L.)*

Right: *Lobbying for cabinet posts in the 1960s which continues to this day! (W.A.L.)*

People stand in long queues in Delhi in the hope of a little sugar—News

Veteran Congress leaders Morarji Desai, Jagjivan Ram, V.K. Krishna Menon, and K.D. Malaviya line up for cabinet berths as Shastri forms his cabinet

THE VOID

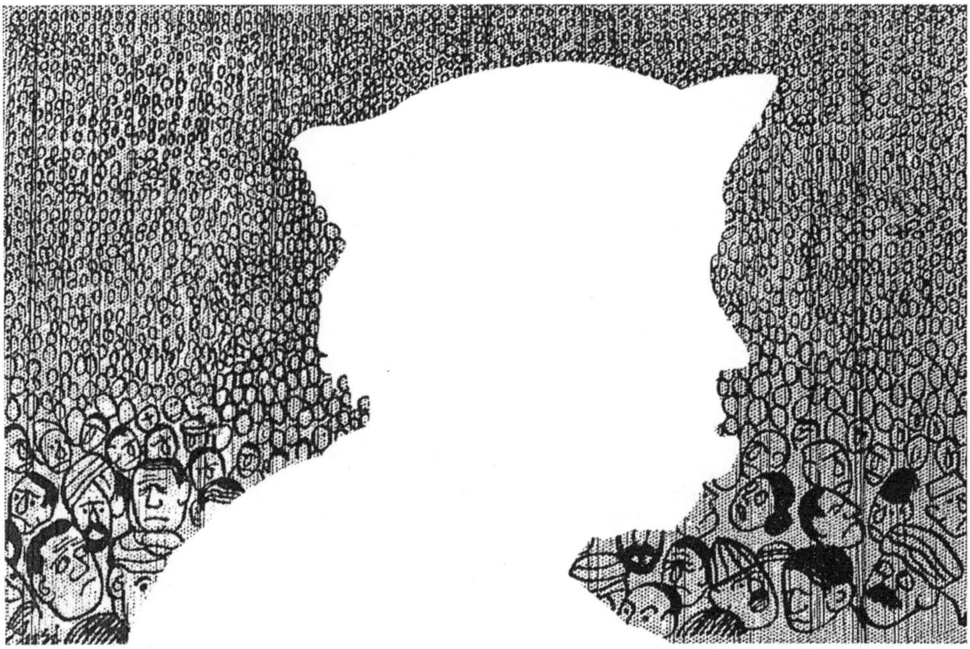

ON THE DEATH OF JAWAHARLAL NEHRU (1889–1964)

Puri's Tribute to Jawaharlal Nehru (1889–1964)

"Das report? Never heard of it—I'm voluntarily resigning because of a UNI report"

Pratap Singh Kairon resigned as Chief Minister of Punjab after the Justice Das Commission indicted him. It was leaked by the national news agency, UNI

"All socialists are welcome to re-enter Congress." —Mr Kamaraj

Some Socialist members led by Asoka Mehta came to the Congress in the mid-1960s. The cartoon shows Kamaraj, Congress President, as a whale swallowing them up

"...And I've fought in the great signature campaigns of '53 '54 '57, '63, '64..."

A politician boasts to an Army veteran (W.A.L.)

Hindustan Times - 15th January 1966

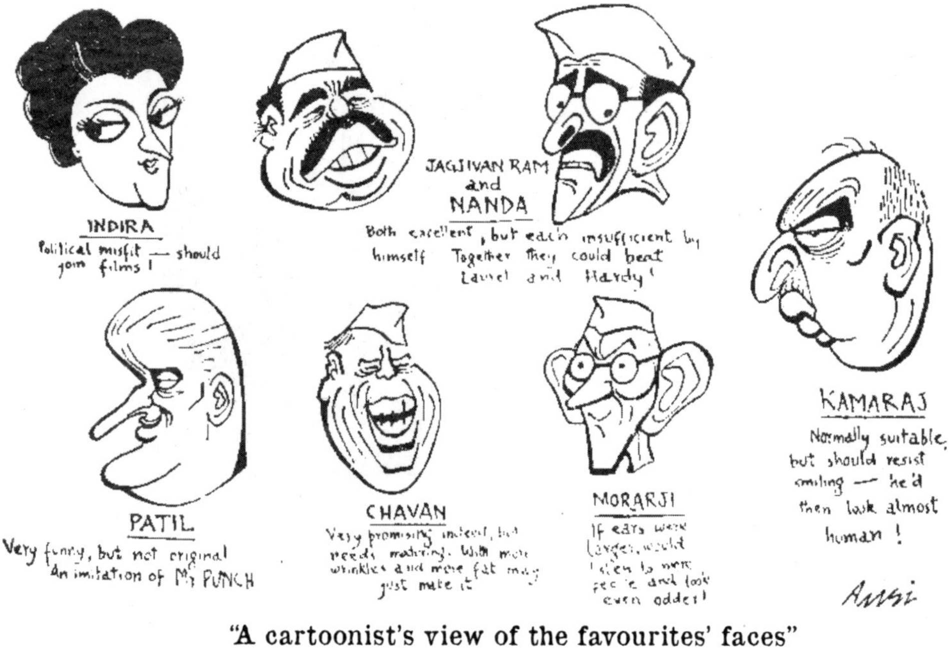

"A cartoonist's view of the favourites' faces"

Right: *After Indira Gandhi defeated Morarji Desai in the Congress leadership contest, Puri drew this cartoon which was published on the front page of* The Hindustan Times *which emphasised the significance of Desai standing on his own against virtually the entire Congress bosses and yet getting 32% of the vote*

Facing page: *On the eve of the election of the successor to Prime Minister Lal Bahadur Shastri in 1966, Puri drew this caricature of the prominent Congress politicians in line for the succession*

Cut down to size?

"But madam, you can't treat a fixed deposit as a current account!"

"I say, does it really matter which planes we buy?"

Above: *Dr Karan Singh, Minister for Civil Aviation and the state of Indian Airlines!*

Facing page: *(above) Morarji Desai faces economic issues as Finance Minister*

(below) Indira Gandhi and Morarji Desai had differences over the nationalisation of banks

"It doesn't belong to me it just happens to like me!"

"SHE DID SAY SHE WAS BEHIND ME..."

Above: *Backstabbing by the Indira Gandhi group of the official Congress nominee in the Presidential Elections, 1969*

Facing page: *President Richard Nixon on his visit to India is given a welcome by Indira Gandhi and communist fellow travellers*

"See? This is what I call an objective cartoon!"

Above: *During the 1969 crisis Indira Gandhi accused Puri of drawing cartoons that were in bad form about her, prompting Puri to produce this cartoon*

Below: *A comment on Mrs Gandhi's appeal for free vote*

There is a, second reaction that the public could give at the next poll. It could vote back Indira to office and thereby give implicit approval to her actions since 1969. The implications of this would be clear. In the expectation of quick, easy prosperity for the masses raised by Indira, the public would have chosen to overlook the political immorality of her government. It would, in that case, be opting for the material rewards contained in her promises and discarding the code of conduct sanctioned by its culture. In effect, the public would have voted for the whimsical morality of a dictator within the disciplined framework of democracy. The result of this would be inevitable. Democracy, without a fight, would very soon give way to dictatorship. What second thoughts the public may entertain within the iron bars of a totalitarian regime are irrelevant to this essay...

A Crisis of Conscience: India 1969

1971–1980

SECTION–II

The dawn of the 1970s was an era of progress as well as disillusionment. After the victory in Bangladesh and of Indira Gandhi in the general elections of 1971, a downward slide began. Through the pages of his own *Stir Weekly* and other publications, Puri unrelentingly hit his targets through his cartoons.

During the internal Emergency of 1975–77, Puri went underground. It was only after the 1977 elections when the Janata Party (of which he was General Secretary) came to power that he resumed drawing caricatures. When the Janata Party split, he sided with the Lok Dal of Charan Singh. In these pages are cartoons of that decade.

Most Indians ceased worrying about this, apparently, centuries ago. In all calculations that all governments and political parties make for organising society, little thought or care seems to be spent on removing beggary from India. There is a reason for that. While the poor do vote, the beggars, stray exceptions apart, don't. Their world is too far removed from ours to afford this luxury. They have no future beyond the next moment, and recognise no divisions, by way of political parties and groups, among the creatures who live under roofs and eat meals every day, twice a day, and have always clothes to wear. . . Our world and the beggar's world don't mix except when alms are given and taken. But the beggars don't seem to hate this—they simply accept it. The tragedy is that so do all of us.

'The Troubled Nation'

(*India, the Wasted Years: 1969–1975*)

"I hear there is something called the CIA—they give money to people..."

In the 1970s it had become commonplace for the government to allege CIA funding for the opposition activities against it

"...And remember—there was no electricity during Ram Rajya either!"

"I know all about the Reserve Bank and the Credit Squeeze, old chap—but just pretend I'm Nagarwala..."

Above: *The Nagarwala case of 1971 was a Bank swindle involving the Prime Minister's name*

Facing page: *The demand for rural electrification was gaining ground*

"Please madam, can I get back *garibi*—I have been miserable ever since it was removed!"

Above: *Puri's parody on the Janata Government of 1977 to 1979*

Facing page: *(above) Indira Gandhi speaking from a tank illustrates her discomfort with the people*

(below) the Garibi Hatao (Remove Poverty) Programme of Indira Gandhi is depicted sarcastically here

1981–1990

SECTION–III

The Janata Government collapsed at the end of the 1970s. 1980 saw the Congress storm to power again with Indira Gandhi at the helm. New problems arose—terrorism in the Punjab, insurgency in Assam, and a general feeling of a lack of direction in the polity at large. Operation Blue Star in the Punjab, the assassination of Indira Gandhi, followed by the horrendous anti-Sikh riots, and the advent of Rajiv Gandhi, who was making an effort to usher in a new form of governance within the present Indian system.

Puri was taking note of all this and not sparing those in power, while drawing cartoons for several newspapers and periodicals.

As may be seen, the Punjab went through turbulent spurts of struggle almost uninterruptedly through the century from Ranjit Singh's death to the transfer of power in 1947. Despite this, an impression in the rest of India is allowed to persist to this day that the Punjab dragged its feet in the quest for freedom, and that Punjabis were more pro-British than the rest. The truth was the other way round.

Out of 2,175 Indian martyrs for freedom, 1,557 or 75% were Sikhs. Out of 2,646 Indians sent to the Andamans for life imprisonment 2,147 or 80% were Sikhs. Out of 127 Indians who were hanged 92 or 80% were Sikhs. Out of 20,000 who joined the Indian National Army under Subhas Bose, 12,000 or 60% were Sikhs.

'Punjab,' *Recovery of India*

In the run-up to the 1984 General Elections Puri thought Rajiv Gandhi and Arun Nehru were the Gandhi and Nehru of the changing times

Mr Clean?

Above: *Rajiv Gandhi on becoming Prime Minister gave an appeal for peace and order even as the lumpen element in the Youth Congress seemed to be up to mischief*

Below: *Despite many independent enquiries indicting Congressmen in the Delhi riots, Rajiv Gandhi initially stonewalled demands for a government enquiry denting his image as 'Mr Clean'*

Rajiv Gandhi soon realised that vested interests were difficult to remove

1991–2000

SECTION-IV

The last decade of the 20th century witnessed a new India taking shape. Coalition politics had become the order of the day. Terrorism in Punjab was ultimately quelled by the middle of the decade. Kashmir was a flash point after the mass exodus of the Kashmiri Pandits from the Valley, which remained under the shadow of the gun. The destruction of the Babri Masjid by *karsevaks* in 1992 was the low point of the decade.

The economic reform process ushered in by the Narasimha Rao–Manmohan Singh duo was also one of the major developments of these years, as we moved towards a market economy. Who better to capture these events with his eagle eye through his cartoons than the inimitable Rajinder Puri, as the years rolled on.

[T]he Home Ministry with characteristic efficiency has informed us that the ISI has smuggled 7,000 trained agents and 61,900 automatic weapons into India. This information weighs heavily on some national leaders.

According to Parliament's Central Hall sources, last week a leader was in his party office when a worker gasped that fire was raging in a city building. 'It must be the ISI,' said the leader.

Another ran in with the news that some factories had gone on strike. 'It's the ISI,' the leader repeated with conviction.

A third came in and said that there was rioting in the neighbourhood. 'I tell you, it's the ISI,' the leader said.

A relative of the leader came in and said, 'Good news, the doctor confirms that your wife is expecting!' 'ISI...!' the leader muttered.'

My, oh my, oh my!
How bravely our police try
To rival the ISI
In making us sob and cry!

23 November 1998, Bull's Eye, *Outlook*

India was open to corporate investment in the 1990s and how!

Half the world believes in violent, bloody revolution, half in peaceful, democratic elections...
..India believes in non-alignment and co-existence..
.. So why not have VIOLENT, BLOODY ELECTIONS!?

"KASHMIR CHOSE GANDHI'S INDIA —NOT JINNAH'S PAKISTAN!"
Ey.. Where is Gandhi's India?

***Above:** The fruitless search for national integration*

***Facing page:** (above) A tie-up the world over for violent elections*

(below) Chandra Shekhar as Prime Minister could not find Gandhi's India

Time to take off your gold bangles, dear!
INDIA
FOREIGN DEBT

How about a Commission to probe why Commissions are appointed?
THAKKAR COMMISSION ON INDIRA MURDER
JAIN COMMISSION ON RAJIV
Ban on publishing proceedings in Rajiv case

Above: *Prime Minister Benazir Bhutto has her eyes on the turmoil in Kashmir even as Sind is on the boil*

Facing page: *(above) Chandra Shekhar was forced to pawn the nation's gold for foreign debt*

(below) S.B. Chavan the Home Minister on the tricky question of commissions of inquiry

When Disneyland was a priority!

How relevant is Independence Day?

P.V. Narasimha Rao could not resolve if the Vote Bank was more imperative to India's growth than the World Bank

A general election often throws up a novel view of genocide

Criminals in politics were a big issue by the 1990s

V.P. Singh's take on sharing power!

2001–2010

SECTION–V

The dawn of the 21st century was unique in India in ways more than one. For the first time a coalition non-Congress government under A.B. Vajpayee completed its full term, followed by a shock defeat at the hands of the Congress-led UPA.

On the flip side, the Gujarat pogrom of 2002, preceded by the Godhra incident shocked the conscience of the nation. India was moving ahead technologically and economically but the scourges of poverty and unemployment were still gnawingly prevalent, 60 years after independence. The Manmohan Singh government won an encore at the hustings in 2009.

The cartoons in these pages show Rajinder Puri had not dimmed his acerbic artistic skills in any measure. By the end of the decade he hung up his cartoonist's brush and bid adieu to the art. A tireless fighter had taken his bow from the field, which had made him a household name.

Fifty-eight passengers died at Godhra. Only four among them were reserved passengers. Nineteen remained unidentified. Thirty-five charred non-reserved passengers, therefore, were 'identified' by the government.

Who were they?

We still don't know this six months after the tragedy.

Is this investigation or farce? Never mind the government, what about the media? Editors have armies of reporters under them. Can't they track down reserved passengers and ask them how and why they were not in the carriage when it was burnt? Or is the truth too frightening to confront?

26 August 2002, Bull's Eye, *Outlook*

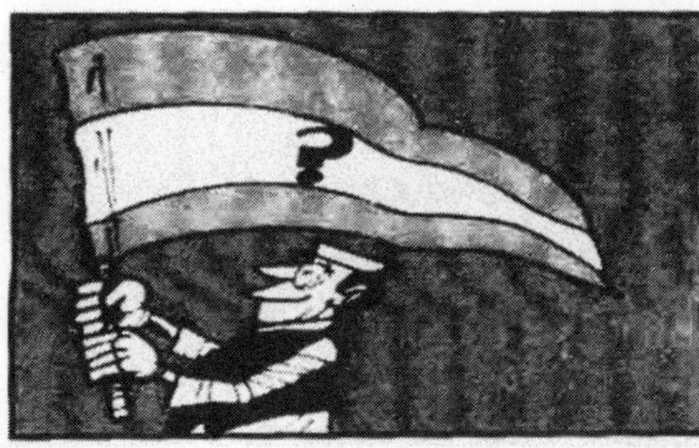

Above: *The misuse of the constitutional power vested with them by politicians prompted Puri to draw this cartoon in his column for* Outlook *magazine*

Below: *Puri often drew cartoons of Narendra Modi then the Chief Minister of Gujarat. This one shows him looking at the world through Hitlerian spectacles*

NEWSHOUND by RAP

NEWSHOUND by RAP

Above and facing page: *Puri also drew a popular cartoon strip called* Newshound *which portrayed a dog. He used the pseudonym Rap for this*

Nuclear programmes of North Korea since 2005

Ongoing conflict between (new) economy and administration—still relevant

Muslim women's rights!

Holding the common man to ransom

The power struggle between M.L. Khurana and L.K. Advani in the BJP

Chaste of character! (L.K. Advani and K.S. Sudarshan, RSS Chief)

Narendra Modi pulled in either direction

Mumbai's annual floods

On the Nanvati Commission report about the 1984 anti-Sikh riots

The perennial conflict between the Judiciary and the polity

Another vision of the 1984 anti-Sikh riots

Bringing in the New Year!

Searching for cabinet jobs

Urban vs Rural

Musharraf on ticking time bomb!

In defence of Indian democracy

The ghosts of the anti-Muslim riots (Gujarat 2002)

'I'll be judge, I'll be jury', said the cunning old Fury (Lewis Carroll)

You have a strong Constitution —but stop abusing your system!
POWER
Republic
Of India – 2006

IX
SCHEDULE
Sealed
Laws

Happy 2-007!

Above: *The Indian Bond!*

Facing page: *(above) The benefits of a strong constitution*

(below) 9th Schedule, the Anti-Defection Law

Public Sector vs Private Sector

The crooked but long arm of the law

Capricious ideology!

The numbers game

Mother and Child

Child of the system—Nithari

Two sides of the same coin—
Punjab politics

The bridge foursome!

Who? Hu!

All in the family

The 'cheer'ful side of parliamentary attendance

The war of the Gills

In Modi`s shadow

Political trickery

Versions of Marx!

Notions of Independence

Two views on Gandhi

The Police College

2006–2010

A cardinal of the Police Service

PM Manmohan Singh's prayers to check inflation

The eternally shortchanged Indian citizen

The dilemma of being a Thackeray!

The fledgling Indian space programme

Liquidity crunch!

A comic misunderstanding of a common name

There are probes and probes!

A most unusual joint family

Above: *Smoking is injurious (Statutory Warning)*

Right: *The eternal wait*

The effects of 26/11/08 terrorist attack on Mumbai

The corrosive power of Indian politics!

Citizen by-passed

Saving Mahatma Gandhi's precious legacy!

Election rhetoric

Abraham Lincoln celebrates the first black president of the USA

2006–2010

Pluralist India and Mr Modi!

Mahatma Gandhi, Haryana style!

L.K. Advani always reached out with political journeys (yatras)

Acknowledgements

We wish to extend our gratitude to Lt. Gen. (Retd) Parikshit Puri for his constant support, as well as to various publications in which Rajinder Puri's cartoons were published: *The Statesman, The Hindustan Times, The Tribune* (Chandigarh), *Outlook* and *The Illustrated Weekly of India* (no longer in print).

Our thanks are also due to *Fountain Ink* where parts of the introductory essay first appeared.

Partha Chatterjee ◆ Arvindar Singh